'THE' Meal Planner

A Year of Meals

Never wonder... "What's for Dinner?"

Take the guesswork out of mealtime & grocery shopping.
Everyone in your family will work as a team in the preparation of meals and grocery shopping.

Lisa Suzanne Hudziak

'THE' Meal Planner
A Year of Meals

Take the guesswork out of mealtime & grocery shopping.
Everyone in your family will work as a team in the preparation of meals and grocery shopping.

Cover designed by Lisa Suzanne Hudziak
Cover - Free Stock Images
ISBN 9 78 1716 58710-8

Dedication:
To My Wonderful Family

How to Use This Planner

I created this planner because grocery shopping happens every week or so whether we like it or not. Meal planning can be very time consuming and after over 20 years of doing it for my family, I was desperate for an easier plan. I have been home for most of the past 23 years as a mother of four wonderful young people and the wife of an amazing husband. I admit, I'm over the shopping and cooking monotony that happens each week and I need to simplify life. For many years, my husband traveled, my kids were too small to cook, but that changed, and I wanted to change with the times. I may be home full-time, but that doesn't make me the maid. I'm part of a team that shares the household responsibilities and this book keeps everyone accountable. As a parent, it's my responsibility to raise useful and responsible adults. I take that very seriously and this book helps in that process.

Making meal preparation a team effort will be so much easier with this book. Everyone will be able to create a grocery list and/or do the grocery shopping. If your home has multiple chefs (teach children to cook), this will make that so much easier. Designate specific days of the week, for different chefs.

This planner is designed to work with all different household schedules. Whether grocery shopping is a daily, weekly, or monthly activity, it'll work for your home. This planner will also be useful for a typical week or an out-of-the-ordinary week, like Thanksgiving or a Super Bowl gathering!

Plan a week, a month or a year of meals and never plan again, unless you want to. Literally, once you create a 'Weekly Meal Plan', you can reuse it as often as you want. I plan to fill in this book, with a year of meals, and never do it again. I'll just open to the week I want, check the kitchen for the necessary supplies, create a shopping list and head to the grocery store. This goes for Thanksgiving too. Since I typically make the same foods each year, I will never have to go back to the recipe books to recreate a meal plan or grocery list ever again. Everything needed, for meal prep and grocery shopping, will be on one page. Reuse favorite recipes during the year, while still creating a variety of different weekly meal plans. Cooking doesn't have to be boring or time consuming.

There are pages for holiday planning as well as weekly planning. These are great for family birthday dinners too! Let's be real, our families like a handful of recipes and many weeks look alike, it takes lots of time to sit down each week, look through recipes, and then write down what I need for each recipe. With this book, I write down what I need for the recipes ONCE and then after taking inventory, I go shopping. What used to take hours of planning, it now only takes minutes.

Grocery Shopping Day, Step-By-Step:
1. Open this book to the week you want to use.
2. Get your grocery shopping list, along with this book, and go through the pantries, fridges, and freezers to see what you need to add to the grocery shopping list.
3. Open the book to page 7, your 'Meals-on-Hand' lists and add needed items to your grocery shopping list.
4. Clip coupons or add coupons to your apps or simply go grocery shopping.

Who can do this? Any family member with a drivers license. We believe in a team-family effort to accomplish household duties. Who can cook dinner? Anyone who's deemed responsible. Keep this book in the kitchen where everyone can see what's for dinner! Maybe your family has a dinner-chef responsibility that goes to the person who gets home first, or everyone takes turns preparing dinner for the family. Everyone can and should learn to cook before moving out on their own, build that strength while you have them at home. Send them out prepared to be successful to cook healthy for themselves and one day their families. The rest of the family can be on clean-up duty. We keep this book open, to our weekly meal plan, and place it on the cookbook holder. When a holiday comes around, let everyone decide which part of the meal they would like to prepare and write their name in pencil next to their choice. Use a pencil for this entire book, just in case you decide you don't like a recipe or to change up the holiday responsibilities. Take one year to create this book and reuse it for the rest of your life or sit down and knock it out over a short period of time and reuse it for the rest of your life. This book was created to be a one-and-done book. No need to ever buy another book. I grocery shop on Thursdays, therefore I make 'Day 1' of the planners Thursday.

To take this meal preparation a step further. Section out your kitchen in meal prep stations. This may sound too detailed or impossible if you have a small kitchen, but we have an older home that has a pretty small kitchen. I have two cookbook stands, one for the baking area and one for the cooking area. The cooking side of the kitchen is next to the stove. The upper cabinet has all the foods that meals use, and the lower cabinets house the pots-and-pans. The drawer has the items used when I cook. Across the kitchen I have our baking area, the upper cabinet filled with baking food supplies and the lower cabinet has the baking pans, with tools in the drawer. The blender/smoothie maker fits in the baking area, so those supplies are all in the baking station. Next to my fridge, the upper cabinet is filled with plates, bowls, and cups. The lower cabinet stores breakfast and lunch foods. The fridge is closest to the table, which is why I decided that's where the meal dishes, utensils, breakfast, and lunch foods would go. The dishwasher is across the kitchen, but it's really not that big of a deal to walk a few feet to put things away. Doing this makes it easier for everyone to make their own breakfast and lunches without traveling all over the kitchen. This also makes dinner time less congested in the kitchen. The person setting the table doesn't cross the path of the chef to set the table. The toaster and waffle iron are by the breakfast station.

Page 12 Notes: Daily Meal 'Type' Planner Use this table to create a general meal plan for regular weeks. Write in, with a pencil; 'breakfast', 'brunch', 'lunch' &/or 'dinner' in the 'Planned Meals' column. Most of us only "cook" one meal each day, this helps you plan for that meal. For example, on Sunday, I make brunch, so I write "Brunch" on Sunday. The actual recipe information will go on the 'Weekly Meal Planner' pages that follow. We still plan to eat the rest of the day, but we'll use leftovers or quick-to-prepare foods found in the 'Meals-on-Hand' list. **Busy Night Tip:** Have a night of the week that's so busy with activities you don't have time to cook? That can be a 'leftovers', 'Meals-on-Hand', 'eat-out' or maybe a 'crock-pot' meal night. Write in the 'type' of meal you need to plan for that night of the week. Title these weeks 'busy or sports weeks' and reuse them when the busy seasons come around each year. If you use a pencil for everything, then you can make changes, as necessary.

'Meals-on-Hand' Planner: Write in, the foods you want to always have in the house, for each particular meal. These are quick-to-make foods that don't need a recipe or much effort to prepare. For example, we always have cereal for breakfast, sandwich fix-in's for lunch and pizza for dinner. When it comes time to make your grocery list, add any items, from these lists, that you're out of. Keep a grocery list notebook in a kitchen drawer and when an item runs out, it can easily be added to the list by the person who used the last of it.

Complete your **"Weekly Meal Planners"**, by using the **Daily Meal 'Type' Planner** from page 12. Decide on the recipe you plan to make, then add the information to this page. Write in the recipe name, cookbook title, page number and preparation time required. Then, at the bottom of the page, log the food items required to make the recipe. You don't need to write in the quantity needed, unless you feel it's significant, like when making a 3lb. roast. This will assist in making your grocery list later. Complete these pages, as far in advance as you decide, but the grocery shopping can wait until the actual week you're on. **Note:** If I plan to serve rice, a salad, some fruit, or dessert with the meal, I write that in too. I always buy fruit, so sometimes I just write fruit on the planner without being specific. This will ensure I have what I need at mealtime without being too specific. Prep-Time should be from start to finish for all the foods being made for a meal. This will tell you when it's time to start or allow you to prepare some of the food the day before, if necessary.

21-day FIX Meal Plan: I DID NOT CREATE THIS DIET PLAN. THE BEACHBODY COMPANY OWNS IT. I CREATED A MEAL PLANNER YEARS AGO AND HAVE ALTERED IT TO INCLUDE THE NOTES FOR ME TO UTILIZE THE 21-DAY FIX MEAL PLAN IN MY DIET. I HAVE NOT COPIED ANY OF THEIR FORMS BUT HAVE CREATED MY SYSTEM AND WORKSHEETS TO ASSIST ME AND MY FAMILY. I'M ADDING IT TO A SPECIAL MEAL PLANNER TO ASSIST THOSE OF US WHO USE BEACHBODY AND MY MEAL PLANNER. AGAIN, I HAVE NOT COPIED ANYTHING BECAUSE I CREATED THE PLANNER MYSELF. IF YOU ARE INTERESTED IN GETTING

IN SHAPE OR LOSEING WEIGHT, I STRONGLY RECOMMEND YOU CHECK OUT WWW.BEACHBODY.COM AND SEE ALL THE GREAT PLANS THEY HAVE TO OFFER. THIS PLANNER IS NOT FROM BEACHBODY. ONE MORE THING, I USE THE 21 DAY TRACKER APP TO LOG MY FOOD. I'VE INCLUDED A WAY TO LOG YOUR ITEMS IN THIS BOOK, BUT YOU CAN USE THE APP TOO.

Portion-control or serving-size diet plans allow our body to be at its healthiest throughout the day. Many healthy eating plans teach that our metabolism is most productive if we refuel our bodies every two and a half to three hours. I have an actual 21-Day FIX Meal Planner, but this is not that. This planner is intended to use a portion-control, serving-size diet to assist with weight management and ease of grocery shopping. If you know your diet plan should have 14 fruits for the week, you can make sure you don't buy more than that. You can plan out your entire week of meals (detailed grocery list) or go to the grocery store with a very simple list. Example

Veggies	21 servings
Fruits	14 servings
Proteins	28 servings
C. Carbs	14 servings
H. Fats	7 servings
Seeds	7 servings
Almond milk	

Use this book to make your life easier. Keep in mind the original planning will be very time-consuming but do it now and you won't have to do it ever again. Once you're at your ideal weight, the plans don't need to change. This planner is created for a single person or a couple. If you need it for more people, I also have a family planner available.

I've added a few 'Helpful Lists' to the back of the book. Having a list of your families 'Favorite Recipes' is always a good idea. If a specific item is hard to find or a bargain at a particular store, the 'Favorite Store' list will come in handy. For items that tend to 'go bad' before their finished, this list can remind you to buy the item in a small size. If there's an item that always seems to 'run out' too quickly, you can buy that in bulk.

Coupon tip: Keep an envelope in the drawer with your grocery list for clipped coupons. Keep flyers, from local car repair shops, miscellaneous stores, and restaurants in this same drawer. Keep a pair of scissors here too. Most stores now have apps that use digital coupons. Add the coupons you plan to use and when you scan your card while shopping, the coupons will be applied and credited automatically.

'Serving-Size' Chart to Achieve 'Portion-Control' Eating Plan

Food Groups	Veggies	Fruits	Proteins	Complex Carbs	Healthy Fats	Seeds & Dressings	Teaspoon	Water
Serving Size	1 Cup	1 Cup	$\frac{3}{4}$ Cup or 3 Ounces	$\frac{1}{2}$ Cup	$\frac{1}{4}$ Cup	2 Tablespoons	1 teaspoon	8 ounces or 1 Cup

Calorie Range Options

Calorie Range	Veggies	Fruits	Proteins	Complex Carbs	Healthy Fats	Seeds & Dressings	Teaspoon	Water
A: 1,200-1,499	3	2	4	2	1	1	3	10
B: 1,500-1,799	4	3	4	3	1	1	4	12
C: 1,800-2,099	5	3	5	4	1	1	5	14
D: 2,100-2,299	6	4	6	4	1	1	6	16
E: 2,300-2,499	7	5	6	5	1	1	7	18
F: 2,500-2,800	8	5	7	5	1	1	8	20

To discover your range, use this website link: https://www.checkyourhealth.org/eat-healthy/cal_calculator.php

'Daily' Total Number of Servings Needed for Each Household Member (Sample)

Household Member Name	Calorie Range	Veggies	Fruits	Proteins	Complex Carbs	Healthy Fats	Seeds & Dressings
1	A	3	2	4	2	1	1
2	B	5	3	5	4	1	1
Daily Totals	NA	16	5	9	6	2	2

'Daily' Total Number of Servings Needed for Each Household Members

Household Member Name	Veggies	Fruits	Proteins	Complex Carbs	Healthy Fats	Seeds & Dressings
Daily Totals						

Once this chart is complete, it will be used as reference point for the weekly grocery planning. You will only need to change it if your calorie range changes.

'Weekly' Total Number of Servings Needed for Each Household Member (Sample)

Household Member Name	Calorie Range	Veggies	Fruits	Proteins	Complex Carbs	Healthy Fats	Seeds & Dressings
1	A	21	14	28	14	7	7
2	B	35	21	35	28	7	7
Weekly Totals	NA	56	35	63	42	14	14

'Weekly' Total Number of Servings Needed for Each Household Members

Household Member Name	Veggies	Fruits	Proteins	Complex Carbs	Healthy Fats	Seeds & Dressings
Weekly Totals						

Once this chart is complete, it will be used as reference point for the weekly grocery planning. You will only need to change it if your calorie range changes.

'Daily' Serving Meal Plan (sample)   Calorie Target Range 1,200-1,499

Time	Meal	Veggies	Fruits	Proteins	Complex Carbs	Healthy Fats	Seeds & Dressings	Teaspoon	Water
Total	Available	4	2	4	2	1	1	3	12
7:30AM	Snack 1		1						2 C
8:30 AM	Breakfast	1	1	1			1	1	2 C
11:00 AM	Snack 2	1							2 C
1:30 PM	Lunch			1	1				2 C.
4:00 PM	Snack 3			1					2 C
6:00 PM	Dinner	1		1	1	1			2 C

Individual Snack Average = ___100___ **calories** (snacks should always be about 100 calories). **Individual Meal Average** = ___300-400___ **calories** (subtract 300 {snack total} from each of the calorie range numbers and then divide by 3 {meals total} to get these numbers).

I have a basic plan of what I know will work for a day, but I adjust it based on what I'm having for dinner that night, I divide out my portions at the start of each day, and then I stick to my plan for that day. Note consider half portions for fruit. My typical day starts with a banana and then a protein-shake after my workout. I try to mix things up a bit, but with limited portions while I lose weight, I'm limited. By having a general plan each day, I can find recipes that work within my plan more easily. Use a pencil because your numbers are going to change.

'Daily' Serving Meal Plan   Calorie Target Range

Time	Meal	Veggies	Fruits	Proteins	Complex Carbs	Healthy Fats	Seeds & Dressings	Teaspoon	Water
Name:									
	Snack 1								
	Breakfast								
	Snack 2								
	Lunch								
	Snack 3								
	Dinner								

Individual Snack Average = __________ **calories** (snacks should always be about 100 calories). **Individual Meal Average** = ______-______ **calories** (subtract snack total from each of the calorie range numbers, then divide by 3 {# of meals}. If you are out and unable to use portion size, use the correct calorie range for your healthiest meal.

'Daily' Serving Meal Plan   Calorie Target Range

Time	Meal	Veggies	Fruits	Proteins	Complex Carbs	Healthy Fats	Seeds & Dressings	Teaspoon	Water
Name:									
	Snack 1								
	Breakfast								
	Snack 2								
	Lunch								
	Snack 3								
	Dinner								

Individual Snack Average = __________ **calories** (snacks should always be about 100 calories). **Individual Meal Average** = ______-______ **calories** (subtract snack total from each of the calorie range numbers, then divide by 3 {# of meals}. If you are out and unable to use portion size, use the correct calorie range for your healthiest meal.

'Daily' Serving Meal Plan   Calorie Target Range

Time	Meal	Veggies	Fruits	Proteins	Complex Carbs	Healthy Fats	Seeds & Dressings	Teaspoon	Water
Name:									
	Snack 1								
	Breakfast								
	Snack 2								
	Lunch								
	Snack 3								
	Dinner								

Individual Snack Average = __________ **calories** (snacks should always be about 100 calories). **Individual Meal Average** = ______-______ **calories** (subtract snack total from each of the calorie range numbers, then divide by 3 {# of meals}. If you are out and unable to use portion size, use the correct calorie range for your healthiest meal.

'Daily' Serving Meal Plan   Calorie Target Range

Time	Meal	Veggies	Fruits	Proteins	Complex Carbs	Healthy Fats	Seeds & Dressings	Teaspoon	Water
Name:									
	Snack 1								
	Breakfast								
	Snack 2								
	Lunch								
	Snack 3								
	Dinner								

Individual Snack Average = _________ calories (snacks should always be about 100 calories). **Individual Meal Average** = ______-______ calories (subtract snack total from each of the calorie range numbers, then divide by 3 {# of meals}. If you are out and unable to use portion size, use the correct calorie range for your healthiest meal.

'Daily' Serving Meal Plan   Calorie Target Range

Time	Meal	Veggies	Fruits	Proteins	Complex Carbs	Healthy Fats	Seeds & Dressings	Teaspoon	Water
Name:									
	Snack 1								
	Breakfast								
	Snack 2								
	Lunch								
	Snack 3								
	Dinner								

Individual Snack Average = _________ calories (snacks should always be about 100 calories). **Individual Meal Average** = ______-______ calories (subtract snack total from each of the calorie range numbers, then divide by 3 {# of meals}. If you are out and unable to use portion size, use the correct calorie range for your healthiest meal.

'Daily' Serving Meal Plan   Calorie Target Range

Time	Meal	Veggies	Fruits	Proteins	Complex Carbs	Healthy Fats	Seeds & Dressings	Teaspoon	Water
Name:									
	Snack 1								
	Breakfast								
	Snack 2								
	Lunch								
	Snack 3								
	Dinner								

Individual Snack Average = _________ calories (snacks should always be about 100 calories). **Individual Meal Average** = ______-______ calories (subtract snack total from each of the calorie range numbers, then divide by 3 {# of meals}. If you are out and unable to use portion size, use the correct calorie range for your healthiest meal.

Recipe Book Recommendations: There are a lot of cookbooks to enjoy for healthy meals. Choose ones that include the nutritional information as well as the number of servings in a recipe. The healthiest diets that I know are included in the list of cookbooks that I'll share next. Keep in mind, these are only a few options, there are lots more out there for your specific needs.

- Fixate & Fixate 2 by Autumn Calabrese (21 Day-FIX),
- The Anti-Inflammatory Diet Cookbook by Madeline Given, NC,
- The Clean Eating Slow Cooker by Linda Larsen
- The 30-Minute Mediterranean Diet Cookbook by Serena Ball & Deanna Segrave-Daly
- Maker's Diet Meals by, Jordan Rubin
- The Daniel Plan Cookbook by Rick Warren, Daniel Amen & Mark Hyman
- The Complete Plant Based Cookbook by America's Test Kitchen

To learn about the 21-Day FIX diet and exercise plan, please read Lose Weight Like Crazy by Autumn Calabrese.

Note: If I plan to serve rice, a salad, some fruit, or dessert with the meal, I write that in too. I always buy fruit, so sometimes I just write fruit on the planner without being specific. This will ensure I have what I need at mealtime without being too specific. Prep-Time should be from start to finish for all the foods being made for a meal. This will tell you when it's time to start or allow you to prepare some of the food the day before, if necessary. Fill in the entire week or do it each day, remember the next time you use this planner, you will not have to do this again. Yahoo!

When you're ready to make your grocery list, fill in this chart. This chart will allow you to make your grocery shopping a little easier without over buying and having food go bad before you can finish it. Tip for veggies or fruit starting to go bad, freeze it and use it in your Protein shakes. You'll use the numbers from the **Weekly Meal Planner** to complete this chart.

1. Count the veggies for breakfast all week and place the number here. Then count the fruits for breakfast all week and place the number on the chart. Do this for breakfast, lunch, dinner, and snacks for the entire week.
2. Add each column individually to get your 'weekly meal planner totals'.
3. Add the 'weekly household servings totals' from the chart on page 7.
4. Subtract the 'weekly meal planner totals', from the 'weekly household servings totals', to get the figures for the 'Additional servings needed totals' line.
5. Write the 'additional servings needed totals' on your grocery list. Pick individual items or keep it general.

Table 1 Sample

Items	Servings Needed
Veggies	6
Fruits	10
Proteins	8
C. Carbs	4
H. Fats	14
Seeds	14

Table 2 Weekly Grocery Numbers at a Glance

Items	Servings Needed
Veggie	
Fruits	
Proteins	
C. Carbs	
H. Fats	
Seeds	

Daily Meal 'Type' Planner

Day	Type: Ethnic, Quick, Large, On-The-Go, Family, Hearty, Leftovers, Healthy…
Sunday	
Monday	
Tuesday	
Wednesday	
Thursday	
Friday	
Saturday	

'Meals-on-Hand' Planner

Breakfast	Lunch	Dinner	Snacks

January: Month At a Glance Planner

Monday	Tuesday	Wednesday	Thursday	Friday	Saturday	Sunday

Monthly Dinner Planner

Date	Recipe Location	Time Required	Grocery Items
	Pg.___		
	Pg.___		
	Pg.___		
	Pg.___		
	Pg.___		
	Pg.___		
	Pg.___		
	Pg.___		
	Pg.___		
	Pg.___		
	Pg.___		
	Pg.___		
	Pg.___		
	Pg.___		
	Pg.___		

Date	Recipe Location	Time Required	Grocery Items
	Pg.___		
	Pg.___		
	Pg.___		
	Pg.___		
	Pg.___		
	Pg.___		
	Pg.___		
	Pg.___		
	Pg.___		
	Pg.___		
	Pg.___		
	Pg.___		
	Pg.___		

Monthly Baking Planner

Date	Item	Recipe Location	Time Required	Grocery Items
		Pg.___		
		Pg.___		
		Pg.___		
		Pg.___		

Family Gathering Meal Planner

Celebration Event Name: _________________________________ Time Meal is Planned For: _____________ am/pm

Course Item	Recipes	cookbook title & page	Prep. Time	Start Time
1:		Pg._____		
2:		Pg._____		
3:		Pg._____		
4:		Pg._____		
5:		Pg._____		
6:		Pg._____		
7:		Pg._____		

4 The Day	Recipes	Cookbook Information	Prep. Time	Start Time
Breakfast		Pg._____		
Lunch		Pg._____		
Dessert		Pg._____		

Foods Needed for Recipes

1:	2:	3:	4:	5:	6:	7:	Breakfast	Lunch	Dessert

February: Month At a Glance Planner

Monday	Tuesday	Wednesday	Thursday	Friday	Saturday	Sunday

Monthly Dinner Planner

Date	Recipe Location	Time Required	Grocery Items
	Pg.___		
	Pg.___		
	Pg.___		
	Pg.___		
	Pg.___		
	Pg.___		
	Pg.___		
	Pg.___		
	Pg.___		
	Pg.___		
	Pg.___		
	Pg.___		
	Pg.___		
	Pg.___		
	Pg.___		
	Pg.___		

Date	Recipe Location	Time Required	Grocery Items
	Pg.___		
	Pg.___		
	Pg.___		
	Pg.___		
	Pg.___		
	Pg.___		
	Pg.___		
	Pg.___		
	Pg.___		
	Pg.___		
	Pg.___		
	Pg.___		
	Pg.___		
	Pg.___		

Monthly Baking Planner

Date	Item	Recipe Location	Time Required	Grocery Items
		Pg.___		
		Pg.___		
		Pg.___		
		Pg.___		

Family Gathering Meal Planner

Celebration Event Name: _________________________________ Time Meal is Planned For: _____________ am/pm

Course Item	Recipes	cookbook title & page	Prep. Time	Start Time
1:		Pg._____		
2:		Pg._____		
3:		Pg._____		
4:		Pg._____		
5:		Pg._____		
6:		Pg._____		
7:		Pg._____		
4 The Day	**Recipes**	**Cookbook Information**	**Prep. Time**	**Start Time**
Breakfast		Pg._____		
Lunch		Pg._____		
Dessert		Pg._____		

Foods Needed for Recipes

1:	2:	3:	4:	5:	6:	7:	Breakfast	Lunch	Dessert

March: Month At a Glance Planner

Monday	Tuesday	Wednesday	Thursday	Friday	Saturday	Sunday

Monthly Dinner Planner

Date	Recipe Location	Time Required	Grocery Items
	Pg.___		
	Pg.___		
	Pg.___		
	Pg.___		
	Pg.___		
	Pg.___		
	Pg.___		
	Pg.___		
	Pg.___		
	Pg.___		
	Pg.___		
	Pg.___		
	Pg.___		
	Pg.___		
	Pg.___		
	Pg.___		

Date	Recipe Location	Time Required	Grocery Items
	Pg.___		
	Pg.___		
	Pg.___		
	Pg.___		
	Pg.___		
	Pg.___		
	Pg.___		
	Pg.___		
	Pg.___		
	Pg.___		
	Pg.___		
	Pg.___		
	Pg.___		

Monthly Baking Planner

Date	Item	Recipe Location	Time Required	Grocery Items
		Pg.___		
		Pg.___		
		Pg.___		
		Pg.___		

Family Gathering Meal Planner

Celebration Event Name: _______________________________ Time Meal is Planned For: _____________ am/pm

Course Item	Recipes	cookbook title & page	Prep. Time	Start Time
1:		Pg._____		
2:		Pg._____		
3:		Pg._____		
4:		Pg._____		
5:		Pg._____		
6:		Pg._____		
7:		Pg._____		
4 The Day	**Recipes**	**Cookbook Information**	**Prep. Time**	**Start Time**
Breakfast		Pg._____		
Lunch		Pg._____		
Dessert		Pg._____		

Foods Needed for Recipes

1:	2:	3:	4:	5:	6:	7:	Breakfast	Lunch	Dessert

April: Month At a Glance Planner

Monday	Tuesday	Wednesday	Thursday	Friday	Saturday	Sunday

Monthly Dinner Planner

Date	Recipe Location	Time Required	Grocery Items
	Pg.___		
	Pg.___		
	Pg.___		
	Pg.___		
	Pg.___		
	Pg.___		
	Pg.___		
	Pg.___		
	Pg.___		
	Pg.___		
	Pg.___		
	Pg.___		
	Pg.___		
	Pg.___		
	Pg.___		
	Pg.___		

Date	Recipe Location	Time Required	Grocery Items
	Pg.___		
	Pg.___		
	Pg.___		
	Pg.___		
	Pg.___		
	Pg.___		
	Pg.___		
	Pg.___		
	Pg.___		
	Pg.___		
	Pg.___		
	Pg.___		
	Pg.___		

Monthly Baking Planner

Date	Item	Recipe Location	Time Required	Grocery Items
		Pg.___		
		Pg.___		
		Pg.___		
		Pg.___		

Family Gathering Meal Planner

Celebration Event Name: _________________________________ Time Meal is Planned For: _____________ am/pm

Course Item	Recipes	cookbook title & page	Prep. Time	Start Time
1:		Pg._____		
2:		Pg._____		
3:		Pg._____		
4:		Pg._____		
5:		Pg._____		
6:		Pg._____		
7:		Pg._____		
4 The Day	**Recipes**	**Cookbook Information**	**Prep. Time**	**Start Time**
Breakfast		Pg._____		
Lunch		Pg._____		
Dessert		Pg._____		

Foods Needed for Recipes

1:	2:	3:	4:	5:	6:	7:	Breakfast	Lunch	Dessert

Family Gathering Meal Planner

Celebration Event Name: _________________________________ Time Meal is Planned For: ______________ am/pm

Course Item	Recipes	cookbook title & page	Prep. Time	Start Time
1:		Pg._____		
2:		Pg._____		
3:		Pg._____		
4:		Pg._____		
5:		Pg._____		
6:		Pg._____		
7:		Pg._____		
4 The Day	**Recipes**	**Cookbook Information**	**Prep. Time**	**Start Time**
Breakfast		Pg._____		
Lunch		Pg._____		
Dessert		Pg._____		

Foods Needed for Recipes

1:	2:	3:	4:	5:	6:	7:	Breakfast	Lunch	Dessert

May: Month At a Glance Planner

Monday	Tuesday	Wednesday	Thursday	Friday	Saturday	Sunday

Monthly Dinner Planner

Date	Recipe Location	Time Required	Grocery Items
	Pg.___		
	Pg.___		
	Pg.___		
	Pg.___		
	Pg.___		
	Pg.___		
	Pg.___		
	Pg.___		
	Pg.___		
	Pg.___		
	Pg.___		
	Pg.___		
	Pg.___		
	Pg.___		
	Pg.___		

Date	Recipe Location	Time Required	Grocery Items
	Pg.___		
	Pg.___		
	Pg.___		
	Pg.___		
	Pg.___		
	Pg.___		
	Pg.___		
	Pg.___		
	Pg.___		
	Pg.___		
	Pg.___		
	Pg.___		
	Pg.___		

Monthly Baking Planner

Date	Item	Recipe Location	Time Required	Grocery Items
		Pg.___		
		Pg.___		
		Pg.___		
		Pg.___		

Family Gathering Meal Planner

Celebration Event Name: _______________________________ Time Meal is Planned For: _____________ am/pm

Course Item	Recipes	cookbook title & page	Prep. Time	Start Time
1:		Pg._____		
2:		Pg._____		
3:		Pg._____		
4:		Pg._____		
5:		Pg._____		
6:		Pg._____		
7:		Pg._____		

4 The Day	Recipes	Cookbook Information	Prep. Time	Start Time
Breakfast		Pg._____		
Lunch		Pg._____		
Dessert		Pg._____		

Foods Needed for Recipes

1:	2:	3:	4:	5:	6:	7:	Breakfast	Lunch	Dessert

Family Gathering Meal Planner

Celebration Event Name: _________________________________ Time Meal is Planned For: _____________ am/pm

Course Item	Recipes	cookbook title & page	Prep. Time	Start Time
1:		Pg._____		
2:		Pg._____		
3:		Pg._____		
4:		Pg._____		
5:		Pg._____		
6:		Pg._____		
7:		Pg._____		

4 The Day	Recipes	Cookbook Information	Prep. Time	Start Time
Breakfast		Pg._____		
Lunch		Pg._____		
Dessert		Pg._____		

Foods Needed for Recipes

1:	2:	3:	4:	5:	6:	7:	Breakfast	Lunch	Dessert

June : Month At a Glance Planner

Monday	Tuesday	Wednesday	Thursday	Friday	Saturday	Sunday

Monthly Dinner Planner

Date	Recipe Location	Time Required	Grocery Items
	Pg.___		
	Pg.___		
	Pg.___		
	Pg.___		
	Pg.___		
	Pg.___		
	Pg.___		
	Pg.___		
	Pg.___		
	Pg.___		
	Pg.___		
	Pg.___		
	Pg.___		
	Pg.___		
	Pg.___		
	Pg.___		

Date	Recipe Location	Time Required	Grocery Items
	Pg.___		
	Pg.___		
	Pg.___		
	Pg.___		
	Pg.___		
	Pg.___		
	Pg.___		
	Pg.___		
	Pg.___		
	Pg.___		
	Pg.___		
	Pg.___		
	Pg.___		
	Pg.___		

Monthly Baking Planner

Date	Item	Recipe Location	Time Required	Grocery Items
		Pg.___		
		Pg.___		
		Pg.___		
		Pg.___		

Family Gathering Meal Planner

Celebration Event Name: _________________________________ Time Meal is Planned For: _____________ am/pm

Course Item	Recipes	cookbook title & page	Prep. Time	Start Time
1:		Pg._____		
2:		Pg._____		
3:		Pg._____		
4:		Pg._____		
5:		Pg._____		
6:		Pg._____		
7:		Pg._____		

4 The Day	Recipes	Cookbook Information	Prep. Time	Start Time
Breakfast		Pg._____		
Lunch		Pg._____		
Dessert		Pg._____		

Foods Needed for Recipes

1:	2:	3:	4:	5:	6:	7:	Breakfast	Lunch	Dessert

July : Month At a Glance Planner

Monday	Tuesday	Wednesday	Thursday	Friday	Saturday	Sunday

Monthly Dinner Planner

Date	Recipe Location	Time Required	Grocery Items
	Pg.___		
	Pg.___		
	Pg.___		
	Pg.___		
	Pg.___		
	Pg.___		
	Pg.___		
	Pg.___		
	Pg.___		
	Pg.___		
	Pg.___		
	Pg.___		
	Pg.___		
	Pg.___		
	Pg.___		
	Pg.___		

Date	Recipe Location	Time Required	Grocery Items
	Pg.___		
	Pg.___		
	Pg.___		
	Pg.___		
	Pg.___		
	Pg.___		
	Pg.___		
	Pg.___		
	Pg.___		
	Pg.___		
	Pg.___		
	Pg.___		
	Pg.___		

Monthly Baking Planner

Date	Item	Recipe Location	Time Required	Grocery Items
		Pg.___		
		Pg.___		
		Pg.___		
		Pg.___		

Family Gathering Meal Planner

Celebration Event Name: ___________________________ Time Meal is Planned For: ___________ am/pm

Course Item	Recipes	cookbook title & page	Prep. Time	Start Time
1:		Pg._____		
2:		Pg._____		
3:		Pg._____		
4:		Pg._____		
5:		Pg._____		
6:		Pg._____		
7:		Pg._____		
4 The Day	**Recipes**	**Cookbook Information**	**Prep. Time**	**Start Time**
Breakfast		Pg._____		
Lunch		Pg._____		
Dessert		Pg._____		

Foods Needed for Recipes

1:	2:	3:	4:	5:	6:	7:	Breakfast	Lunch	Dessert

Family Gathering Meal Planner

Celebration Event Name: _________________________________ Time Meal is Planned For: _____________ am/pm

Course Item	Recipes	cookbook title & page	Prep. Time	Start Time
1:		Pg._____		
2:		Pg._____		
3:		Pg._____		
4:		Pg._____		
5:		Pg._____		
6:		Pg._____		
7:		Pg._____		
4 The Day	Recipes	Cookbook Information	Prep. Time	Start Time
Breakfast		Pg._____		
Lunch		Pg._____		
Dessert		Pg._____		

Foods Needed for Recipes

1:	2:	3:	4:	5:	6:	7:	Breakfast	Lunch	Dessert

August: Month At a Glance Planner

Monday	Tuesday	Wednesday	Thursday	Friday	Saturday	Sunday

Monthly Dinner Planner

Date	Recipe Location	Time Required	Grocery Items
	Pg.___		
	Pg.___		
	Pg.___		
	Pg.___		
	Pg.___		
	Pg.___		
	Pg.___		
	Pg.___		
	Pg.___		
	Pg.___		
	Pg.___		
	Pg.___		
	Pg.___		
	Pg.___		
	Pg.___		
	Pg.___		
	Pg.___		

Date	Recipe Location	Time Required	Grocery Items
	Pg.___		
	Pg.___		
	Pg.___		
	Pg.___		
	Pg.___		
	Pg.___		
	Pg.___		
	Pg.___		
	Pg.___		
	Pg.___		
	Pg.___		
	Pg.___		
	Pg.___		

Monthly Baking Planner

Date	Item	Recipe Location	Time Required	Grocery Items
		Pg.___		
		Pg.___		
		Pg.___		
		Pg.___		

Family Gathering Meal Planner

Celebration Event Name: _______________________________________ Time Meal is Planned For: _______________ am/pm

Course Item	Recipes	cookbook title & page	Prep. Time	Start Time
1:		Pg._____		
2:		Pg._____		
3:		Pg._____		
4:		Pg._____		
5:		Pg._____		
6:		Pg._____		
7:		Pg._____		

4 The Day	Recipes	Cookbook Information	Prep. Time	Start Time
Breakfast		Pg._____		
Lunch		Pg._____		
Dessert		Pg._____		

Foods Needed for Recipes

1:	2:	3:	4:	5:	6:	7:	Breakfast	Lunch	Dessert

September: Month At a Glance Planner

Monday	Tuesday	Wednesday	Thursday	Friday	Saturday	Sunday

Monthly Dinner Planner

Date	Recipe Location	Time Required	Grocery Items
	Pg.___		
	Pg.___		
	Pg.___		
	Pg.___		
	Pg.___		
	Pg.___		
	Pg.___		
	Pg.___		
	Pg.___		
	Pg.___		
	Pg.___		
	Pg.___		
	Pg.___		
	Pg.___		
	Pg.___		

Date	Recipe Location	Time Required	Grocery Items
	Pg.___		
	Pg.___		
	Pg.___		
	Pg.___		
	Pg.___		
	Pg.___		
	Pg.___		
	Pg.___		
	Pg.___		
	Pg.___		
	Pg.___		
	Pg.___		
	Pg.___		
	Pg.___		

Monthly Baking Planner

Date	Item	Recipe Location	Time Required	Grocery Items
		Pg.___		
		Pg.___		
		Pg.___		
		Pg.___		

Family Gathering Meal Planner

Celebration Event Name: ___________________________ Time Meal is Planned For: ___________ am/pm

Course Item	Recipes	cookbook title & page	Prep. Time	Start Time
1:		Pg._____		
2:		Pg._____		
3:		Pg._____		
4:		Pg._____		
5:		Pg._____		
6:		Pg._____		
7:		Pg._____		
4 The Day	**Recipes**	**Cookbook Information**	**Prep. Time**	**Start Time**
Breakfast		Pg._____		
Lunch		Pg._____		
Dessert		Pg._____		

Foods Needed for Recipes

1:	2:	3:	4:	5:	6:	7:	Breakfast	Lunch	Dessert

Family Gathering Meal Planner

Celebration Event Name: _________________________________ Time Meal is Planned For: _______________ am/pm

Course Item	Recipes	cookbook title & page	Prep. Time	Start Time
1:		Pg._____		
2:		Pg._____		
3:		Pg._____		
4:		Pg._____		
5:		Pg._____		
6:		Pg._____		
7:		Pg._____		

4 The Day	Recipes	Cookbook Information	Prep. Time	Start Time
Breakfast		Pg._____		
Lunch		Pg._____		
Dessert		Pg._____		

Foods Needed for Recipes

1:	2:	3:	4:	5:	6:	7:	Breakfast	Lunch	Dessert

October: Month At a Glance Planner

Monday	Tuesday	Wednesday	Thursday	Friday	Saturday	Sunday

Monthly Dinner Planner

Date	Recipe Location	Time Required	Grocery Items
	Pg.___		
	Pg.___		
	Pg.___		
	Pg.___		
	Pg.___		
	Pg.___		
	Pg.___		
	Pg.___		
	Pg.___		
	Pg.___		
	Pg.___		
	Pg.___		
	Pg.___		
	Pg.___		
	Pg.___		
	Pg.___		

Date	Recipe Location	Time Required	Grocery Items
	Pg.___		
	Pg.___		
	Pg.___		
	Pg.___		
	Pg.___		
	Pg.___		
	Pg.___		
	Pg.___		
	Pg.___		
	Pg.___		
	Pg.___		
	Pg.___		

Monthly Baking Planner

Date	Item	Recipe Location	Time Required	Grocery Items
		Pg.___		
		Pg.___		
		Pg.___		
		Pg.___		

Family Gathering Meal Planner

Celebration Event Name: _______________________________ Time Meal is Planned For: _______________ am/pm

Course Item	Recipes	cookbook title & page	Prep. Time	Start Time
1:		Pg._____		
2:		Pg._____		
3:		Pg._____		
4:		Pg._____		
5:		Pg._____		
6:		Pg._____		
7:		Pg._____		
4 The Day	**Recipes**	**Cookbook Information**	**Prep. Time**	**Start Time**
Breakfast		Pg._____		
Lunch		Pg._____		
Dessert		Pg._____		

Foods Needed for Recipes

1:	2:	3:	4:	5:	6:	7:	Breakfast	Lunch	Dessert

Family Gathering Meal Planner

Celebration Event Name: _______________________ Time Meal is Planned For: _____________ am/pm

Course Item	Recipes	cookbook title & page	Prep. Time	Start Time
1:		Pg.______		
2:		Pg.______		
3:		Pg.______		
4:		Pg.______		
5:		Pg.______		
6:		Pg.______		
7:		Pg.______		
4 The Day	**Recipes**	**Cookbook Information**	**Prep. Time**	**Start Time**
Breakfast		Pg.______		
Lunch		Pg.______		
Dessert		Pg.______		

Foods Needed for Recipes

1:	2:	3:	4:	5:	6:	7:	Breakfast	Lunch	Dessert

November: Month At a Glance Planner

Monday	Tuesday	Wednesday	Thursday	Friday	Saturday	Sunday

Monthly Dinner Planner

Date	Recipe Location	Time Required	Grocery Items
	Pg.___		
	Pg.___		
	Pg.___		
	Pg.___		
	Pg.___		
	Pg.___		
	Pg.___		
	Pg.___		
	Pg.___		
	Pg.___		
	Pg.___		
	Pg.___		
	Pg.___		
	Pg.___		
	Pg.___		
	Pg.___		

Date	Recipe Location	Time Required	Grocery Items
	Pg.___		
	Pg.___		
	Pg.___		
	Pg.___		
	Pg.___		
	Pg.___		
	Pg.___		
	Pg.___		
	Pg.___		
	Pg.___		
	Pg.___		
	Pg.___		
	Pg.___		

Monthly Baking Planner

Date	Item	Recipe Location	Time Required	Grocery Items
		Pg.___		
		Pg.___		
		Pg.___		
		Pg.___		

December: Month At a Glance Planner

Monday	Tuesday	Wednesday	Thursday	Friday	Saturday	Sunday

Monthly Dinner Planner

Date	Recipe Location	Time Required	Grocery Items
	Pg.___		
	Pg.___		
	Pg.___		
	Pg.___		
	Pg.___		
	Pg.___		
	Pg.___		
	Pg.___		
	Pg.___		
	Pg.___		
	Pg.___		
	Pg.___		
	Pg.___		
	Pg.___		
	Pg.___		
	Pg.___		

Date	Recipe Location	Time Required	Grocery Items
	Pg.___		
	Pg.___		
	Pg.___		
	Pg.___		
	Pg.___		
	Pg.___		
	Pg.___		
	Pg.___		
	Pg.___		
	Pg.___		
	Pg.___		
	Pg.___		
	Pg.___		

Monthly Baking Planner

Date	Item	Recipe Location	Time Required	Grocery Items
		Pg.___		
		Pg.___		
		Pg.___		
		Pg.___		

Family Gathering Meal Planner

Celebration Event Name: _______________________________ Time Meal is Planned For: _______________ am/pm

Course Item	Recipes	cookbook title & page	Prep. Time	Start Time
1:		Pg._____		
2:		Pg._____		
3:		Pg._____		
4:		Pg._____		
5:		Pg._____		
6:		Pg._____		
7:		Pg._____		

4 The Day	Recipes	Cookbook Information	Prep. Time	Start Time
Breakfast		Pg._____		
Lunch		Pg._____		
Dessert		Pg._____		

Foods Needed for Recipes

1:	2:	3:	4:	5:	6:	7:	Breakfast	Lunch	Dessert

Family Gathering Meal Planner

Celebration Event Name: ________________________________ Time Meal is Planned For: ____________ am/pm

Course Item	Recipes	cookbook title & page	Prep. Time	Start Time
1:		Pg._____		
2:		Pg._____		
3:		Pg._____		
4:		Pg._____		
5:		Pg._____		
6:		Pg._____		
7:		Pg._____		

4 The Day	Recipes	Cookbook Information	Prep. Time	Start Time
Breakfast		Pg._____		
Lunch		Pg._____		
Dessert		Pg._____		

Foods Needed for Recipes

1:	2:	3:	4:	5:	6:	7:	Breakfast	Lunch	Dessert

Family Gathering Meal Planner

Celebration Event Name: _________________________________Time Meal is Planned For: _______________ am/pm

Course Item	Recipes	cookbook title & page	Prep. Time	Start Time
1:		Pg._____		
2:		Pg._____		
3:		Pg._____		
4:		Pg._____		
5:		Pg._____		
6:		Pg._____		
7:		Pg._____		
4 The Day	**Recipes**	**Cookbook Information**	**Prep. Time**	**Start Time**
Breakfast		Pg._____		
Lunch		Pg._____		
Dessert		Pg._____		

Foods Needed for Recipes

1:	2:	3:	4:	5:	6:	7:	Breakfast	Lunch	Dessert

Helpful Lists

Favorite Recipes

Recipe Name	Cookbook Title & Page Number	Preparation Time-Required

Favorite Store for A Special Item

Item	Store	Cost
		$
		$
		$
		$
		$
		$
		$
		$

'Go-Bad' Items: Buy A Small Container Because We Hardly Use It.

Item	Favorite Store to Buy It At	Best Size

'Run-Out' Items: So Good, Buy in Bulk If Possible.

Item	Favorite Store to Buy It At	Best Size